Catholic Prayers: Book 4

Traditional Text

Bright Reads Books is *not* the original author of books it publishes.

Our mission is to reformat public domain text in gigantic fonts—so that visually challenged readers can hold real books and read.

Exclusive, Gigantic 80-Point Type

Offered by:

Bright Reads Books

In Gigantic Print

www.bright-reads-books.com

Find more on Facebook

Anima Christi

Soul of Christ, sanctify me. Body of

Christ, save me.
Blood of Christ, inebriate me. Water from the side of

Christ, cleanse me. Passion of Christ, strengthen me.

O good Jesus, hear me.
Within thy sacred wounds, hide me.

Never suffer me to be separated from Thee. From the malice of my enemies,

defend me.
At the hour
of my death,
call me.
Command
me to come
to Thee,

that with thy
saints I may
praise Thee
for ever and
ever.
Amen.

—St Ignatius Loyola

To Mary

Dearest Mother, I consecrate myself entirely to

you today,
and in order
that I may
always be
close to your
side, I
earnestly

beseech you
to take entire
possession
of my heart
and all my
senses. Never

permit me to
be defiled by
any impure
thoughts or
desires; but
if they
should come

upon me,
stretch forth
your arms
and take me
under your
blue mantle.
Fill my heart

with your
love and
flood all my
senses with
your purity,
that I may
live and die

an
immaculate
son (or
daughter) of
you, my
Immaculate
Mother,

through Christ our Lord. *Amen*.

To Saint Joseph

Saint Joseph, father and guardian of virgins, into

your faithful
keeping
were
entrusted
Innocence
itself, Christ
Jesus, and

Mary, the
Virgin of
virgins. I
pray and
beseech you,
to keep me
from all

unclean-
ness, and to
grant that
my mind
may be
untainted,
my heart

pure and my body chaste. Help me always to serve Jesus and Mary in perfect

chastity.
Amen.

Come, Holy Spirit

Come, Holy Spirit, fill the hearts of thy faithful,

and kindle
within them
the fire of
thy divine
love.

Send forth
Your Spirit
and they
shall be
created. And
Thou shall
renew the

face of the earth.

Let us pray:
O God, You have taught the hearts of

your faithful by the light of the Holy Spirit; grant that by the gift of that same Holy

Spirit we may be truly wise and always rejoice in his con-solation. We ask this

through
Christ our
Lord.

Amen.

"At Bright Reads Books, our editors endeavor to maximize the text's font size for readers. That means we may not be able to consistently or ideally present word breaks, page breaks, punctuation, and other elements of style and grammar. Our priority is making the print easy to read."